creepy creatures

Published by Creative Education
P.O. Box 227, Mankato, Minnesota 56002
Creative Education is an imprint of
The Creative Company
www.thecreativecompany.us

Design by Ellen Huber
Production by Chelsey Luther
Art direction by Rita Marshall
Printed in the United States of America

Photographs by Dreamstime (Melinda Fawver,
Isselee, David Kelly, Ryszard Laskowski, Jens Stolt,
Tzooka), iStockphoto (alxpin, Antagain, Evgeniy
Ayupov, Melinda Fawver, Eric Isselée, TommyIX),
Shutterstock (Miles Boyer, Igor Chernomorchenko,
Coprid, hwongcc, Eric Isselee, Cosmin Manci,
Michael G Smith, Steyno&Stitch, Nuttapong
Wongcheronkit), SuperStock (Biosphoto, Minden
Pictures, NaturePL, Steve Bloom Images, Jochen
Tack/imagebrok/imagebroker.net)

Library of Congress Cataloging-in-Publication Data
Bodden, Valerie.
Moths / Valerie Bodden.
p. cm. — (Creepy creatures)
Summary: A basic introduction to moths, examining
where they live, how they grow, what they eat, and
the traits that help to define them, such as their
transformation from caterpillars to winged insects.
Includes bibliographical references and index.
ISBN 978-1-60818-358-6
1. Moths—Juvenile literature. I. Title. II. Series:
Bodden, Valerie. Creepy creatures.
QL544.2.B496 2014
595.78—dc23   2013009755

First Edition
9 8 7 6 5 4 3 2 1

CONTENTS

Introduction 4

What Is a Moth? 6

A Moth's Life 14

Make a Moth Caterpillar 22

Glossary 23

Read More 24

Websites 24

Index 24

moths

VALERIE BODDEN

CREATIVE ✿ EDUCATION

You are in your backyard at night. Lots of bugs fly around an outdoor light. One has big wings. You look closer.

It is a moth!

Moths are insects. They have three body parts and six legs. Moths have two pairs of wings. Many moths have brown or gray wings. But some are bright colors. Moths have two **antennae** (*an-TEH-nee*) that look like feathers or combs.

The colorful Indian moon moth (right) has large, feathery antennae

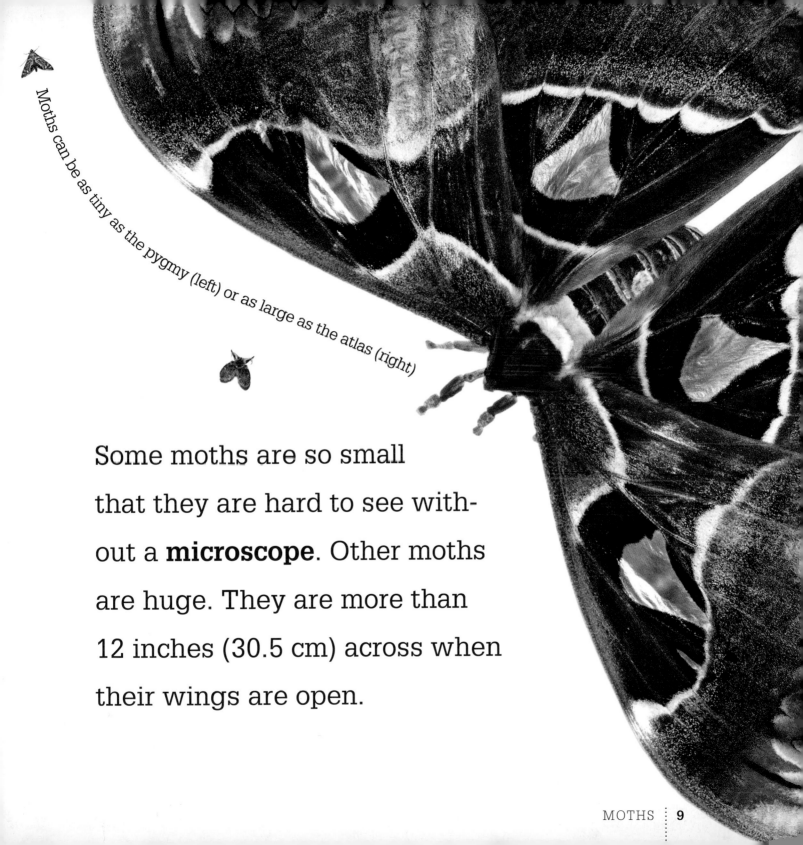

Moths can be as tiny as the pygmy (left) or as large as the atlas (right)

Some moths are so small that they are hard to see without a **microscope**. Other moths are huge. They are more than 12 inches (30.5 cm) across when their wings are open.

There are about 160,000 kinds of moths! Great tiger moths are common in parts of North America. They are brown, white, and orange. Luna moths are found in North America, too. They have light green wings.

An adult luna moth (above) lives for only one week

The garden tiger moth is a European relative of the great tiger moth

Other flying creatures such as birds and bats like to eat moths

Moths live in rainforests, grasslands, and woodlands. Many moths live in cities, too. Moths have to watch out for **predators**. Dragonflies, birds, and bats all eat moths.

Moths begin life in an egg. A **larva** called a caterpillar comes out of the egg. The caterpillar eats a lot of plants. It gets too big for its skin and **molts**. Then the caterpillar stops eating. It becomes a **pupa**. Many pupae have a silk covering called a cocoon around them. An adult moth comes out of the cocoon. Most adult moths live only a few weeks.

A moth can be a pupa (right) for weeks, months, or sometimes years

A moth caterpillar is very small when it first comes out of the egg

Some moths use a long mouthpart called a proboscis (pro-BAH-sis) to drink from flowers

Some adult moths do not eat at all. Others suck up a sugary liquid made by flowers. Some eat rotting fruit or honey. Many moths are active at night.

Some adult moths can fly very fast. Others blend in with the grass or trees around them. Some moths have bright colors or **eyespots** on their back wings to scare away predators.

Moths with eyespots can surprise a predator when they open their wings

Some moths can use their coloration to hide from predators

People who collect moths are called lepidopterists (lep-ih-DAHP-tare-ists)

Some people used to think that if a moth came into their home, it meant someone would die. Other people thought moths were ghosts of dead people. Today, many people collect moths. It can be fun to look at these winged creepy creatures!

MAKE A MOTH CATERPILLAR

You can make your own caterpillar using the bottom of an egg carton. Cut the carton in half the long way so that you can make two caterpillars. Turn one half upside down and paint the bottom. Cut a pipe cleaner into two pieces. Poke each piece into the caterpillar's head. When it is time for the caterpillar to become a moth, cut out some paper wings and glue them on!

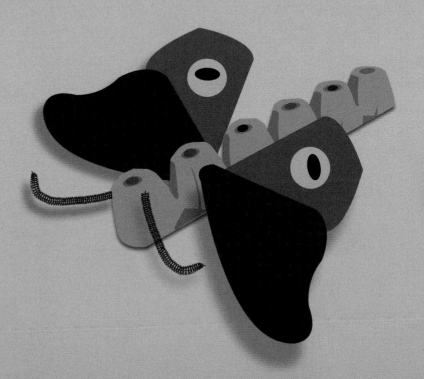

GLOSSARY

antennae: feelers on the heads of some insects that are used to touch, smell, and taste things

eyespots: markings on a moth's wings that look like eyes

larva: the form some insects and animals take when they hatch from eggs, before changing into their adult form

microscope: a machine with special lenses that makes it possible to see very small things

molts: loses a shell or layer of skin and grows a new, larger one

predators: animals that kill and eat other animals

pupa: an insect that is changing from a larva into an adult, usually while inside a covering or case to keep it safe

READ MORE

Hibbert, Clare. *Butterflies and Moths*. Mankato, Minn.: Arcturus, 2011.

Rustad, Martha E. H. *Moths*. Minneapolis: Bellwether Media, 2008.

WEBSITES

BioKIDS: Butterflies and Moths
http://www.biokids.umich.edu/critters/
Lepidoptera/pictures/
Check out pictures of all kinds of butterflies and moths.

Enchanted Learning: Luna Moth
http://www.enchantedlearning.com/
subjects/butterfly/activities/printouts/
Lunamothprintout.shtml
Learn more about luna moths, and print out a picture to color.

INDEX

antennae **6**

caterpillars **14**

cocoons **14**

colors **6, 10, 18**

eyespots **18**

foods **14, 17**

homes **13**

kinds **10**

microscopes **9**

molting **14**

predators **13, 18**

pupae **14**

sizes **9**

wings **4, 6, 9, 10, 21**